FRENCH POLISHING
FOR BEGINNERS

EASY TO FOLLOW STEP BY
STEP INSTRUCTIONS TO
FRENCH POLISH AT HOME

BY

W. A. G. BRADMAN

British Library Cataloguing-in-Publication Data
A catalogue record for this book is available from the
British Library

CONTENTS

Wood Finishing

Wood finishing refers to the process of refining or protecting a wooden surface, especially in the production of furniture. Along with stone, mud and animal parts, wood was one of the first materials worked by early humans. There are incredibly early examples of woodwork, evidenced in Mousterian stone tools used by Neanderthal man, which demonstrate our affinity with the wooden medium. The very development of civilisation is linked to the advancement of increasingly greater degrees of skill in working with these materials. Although it may at first seem a relatively small genre of the 'woodworking canon', wood finishing is an integral part of both structural and decorative aspects of wood work.

Wood finishing starts with sanding, either by hand (typically using a sanding block or power sander), scraping, or planing. When planing, a specialised 'hand plane' tool is required; used to flatten, reduce the thickness of, and impart a smooth surface to a rough piece of lumber or timber. When powered by electricity, the tool may be called a *planer,* and special types of planes are designed to be able to cut joints or decorative mouldings. Hand planes are generally the combination of a cutting edge, such as a sharpened metal plate, attached to a firm body, that when moved over a wood surface, take up relatively uniform shavings. This happens because of the nature of the body riding on the 'high spots' in the wood, and also by providing a relatively constant angle to the cutting edge, render the planed surface very smooth.

When finishing wood, it is imperative to first make sure that it has been adequately cleaned, removing any dust, shavings or residue. Subsequently, if there are any obvious damages or dents in the furniture, wood putty or filler should be used to fill the gaps. Imperfections or nail holes on the surface may be filled using wood putty (also called plastic wood; a substance commonly used to fill nail holes in wood prior to finishing. It is often composed of wood dust combined with a binder that dries and a diluent (thinner), and sometimes, pigment). Filler is normally used for an all over smooth-textured finish, by filling pores in the wood grain. It is used particularly on open grained woods such as oak, mahogany and walnut where building up multiple layers of standard wood finish is ineffective or impractical.

Grain fillers generally consist of three basic components; a binder, a bulking agent and a solvent. The binder is wood finish, and in the case of oil-based fillers is typically a blend of oil and varnish. The type of binder then influences the type of solvent used; oil-based fillers usually use mineral spirits, while water-based fillers (unsurprisingly) use water.

Both types of filler use silica as a bulking agent as it resists shrinking and swelling in response to changes in temperature and humidity. Once the wood surface is fully prepared and stained (or bleached), the finish is applied. It usually consists of several coats of wax, shellac, drying oil, lacquer, varnish, or paint, and each coat is typically followed by sanding. Finally, the surface may be polished or buffed using steel wool, pumice, rotten stone or other materials, depending on the shine desired. Often, a final coat of wax is applied over the finish to add a degree of protection.

There are three major types of finish:

Evaporative - i.e. wax, because it is dissolved in turpentine or petroleum distillates to form a soft paste. After these distillates evaporate, a wax residue is left over.

Reactive - i.e. white spirits or naptha, as well as oil varnishes such as linseed oil - they change chemically when they cure, unlike evaporative finishes. The solvent evaporates and a chemical reaction occurs causing the resins to undergo a change. Linseed oil cures by reacting with oxygen, but does not form a film.

Coalescing - i.e. Water based finishes; a combination of evaporative and reactive finishes, essentially emulsions with slow-evaporating thinners.

French polishing (an evaporative finish) is one of the most widely practiced, and highly respected wood finishing techniques, as it results in a very high gloss surface, with a deep colour and chatoyancy. The technique of applying shellac by rubbing it onto the furniture with a 'rubber' is widely regarded to have begun in France in the early 1800's, hence the description 'French Polish'. This procedure consists of applying many thin coats of shellac, dissolved in alcohol using a rubbing pad lubricated with oil. The rubbing pad is made of absorbent cotton or wool cloth wadding inside a square piece of fabric (usually soft cotton cloth) and is commonly referred to as a *fad*, also called a rubber, or *muñeca*, Spanish for 'rag doll'. It should be noted however, that 'French polish' is a process, not a material. The main material is shellac, although there are several other shellac-based finishes, not all of which class as French polishing. 'Lac' is a natural substance that is the secretion of the Lac insect 'Laccifer lacca', which is found on certain tress principally in the provinces of India and Thailand. The protective coating secreted by the lac insect is a yellow to reddish resin, which is heated, then purified and dried into sheets or flakes for commercial use.

In the Victorian era, French polishing was commonly used on mahogany and other expensive woods. It was considered the best finish for fine furniture and string instruments such as pianos and guitars. The process was very labour intensive though, and many manufacturers abandoned the technique around 1930, preferring the cheaper and quicker techniques of spray finishing nitrocellulose lacquer and abrasive buffing. In Britain, instead of abrasive buffing, a fad of 'pullover' is used in much the same way as traditional French polishing. This slightly melts the sprayed surface and has the effect of filling the grain and burnishing at the same time to leave a 'French polished' look.

Ammonia fuming (reactive) is another traditional process, but in this case, used primarily for darkening and enriching the colour of white oak. Ammonia fumes react with the natural tannins in the wood and cause it to change colour, as well as bringing out the grain pattern; the resultant product known as 'fumed oak'. The process specifically consists of exposing the wood to fumes from a strong aqueous solution of ammonium hydroxide, and can be used on other species of wood, although they will not darken to such an extent. The introduction of the method is usually associated with the American furniture maker, design leader and publisher, Gustav Stickley at the beginning of the twentieth century, but fuming was certainly known in Europe some time before this.

As is evident from this incredibly brief overview of wood finishing techniques, it is an incredibly varied and exciting genre of professional trade and individual art; a traditional craft, still relevant in the modern day. Woodworkers range from hobbyists, individuals operating from the home environment, to artisan professionals with specialist workshops, and eventually large-scale factory operations. We hope the reader is inspired by this book to create and finish some woodwork of their own.

FRENCH POLISHING - I

STAINING AND FILLING

As a surface finish for furniture work, french polishing is unsurpassed. Providing it has been properly applied and that an occasional polishing with furniture cream is given, it will last indefinitely. The passing years merely bring a mellow depth and richness unequalled by any other finish.

For some reason the processes involved in french polishing furniture are, to most people, wrapped in mystery. The opinion is often expressed that unless one knows the art and has learned the tricks of the trade from some hoary old gentleman who has spent his life at the polishing bench, it is hopeless to expect the amateur to do the job. Very well, let us do a little de-bunking!

There *is* an art in french polishing—so there is in sweeping a chimney, washing dishes, laying paving stones or feeding a baby!

There is no mystery about french polishing—merely the methodical application of logical processes.

What 'tricks of the trade' there are, will be covered in the following pages.

And that is all!

Stages in French Polishing.

In general, french polishing is done in seven stages, although one or more may be omitted according to circumstances. The first six are, in their order of working, as follows:—

> Staining.
>
> Filling the Grain.
>
> Fadding.
>
> Colouring.
>
> Coating.
>
> Bodying.

The finishing stage is either stiffing, spiriting off or acid finishing and each will be described later. To make a good job of french polishing the stages must be correctly worked, each being satisfactorily completed before the next is started. It will of course be realised that a certain amount of skill is required and this can only be developed by actual practice. It is better to do the work on a 'practice' piece of wood rather than to wait until you are ready to polish an actual item of furniture. The practice piece should be fairly large so that there is plenty of room in which to work the rubber—(and therefore good opportunities to miss parts of the surface!). A good scheme to follow is to use two practice pieces, one a length of board about three feet long by 6 inches or so wide—(wider if possible), and a piece of plywood about two feet square. With these two pieces to work on you should easily develop the necessary skill and confidence with which to tackle 'serious' work.

It seems hardly necessary to say that french polishing should always be done in a dust-free atmosphere. It is also an advantage to have the room or workshop warm as the polish will flow much more easily under these conditions. The bench should be arranged in front of a window so that when working, the surface can be viewed against the light. By tilting the head sideways and looking across the work towards the light, any streaks can be easily seen and the path of the rubber will show up quite plainly. When looking straight down on the work it is often difficult to see just where the rubber has passed.

STAINING THE WOOD.

Furniture is often polished without any preliminary staining, though it is more usual to do so when french polish is to be used. There are two main reasons for using stain, first to darken the work to a shade which will give better wear than the natural light colour, secondly to bring the whole job to an equal colour even when different varieties of the same wood have been used, and also to bring out the full beauty of the grain.

It must be realised at the outset that no stain can be specifically guaranteed to produce a certain exact shade unless all the facts are known regarding the timber which is being used. Thus different varieties of a particular timber often produce different shades though the same stain is used. To guard against this difficulty it is always advisable to stain a test piece of the actual timber which is to be used and thus to determine the exact strength and mixture of stain which will be required.

Wood may be brought to the required colour by four main processes, i.e., water stains, spirit stains, oil stains and fuming. Let us consider each in turn.

Water Stains.

This type of stain is the most frequently used on account of its cheapness, good penetration, clarity of colour and exceptional covering capacity. It is made by mixing water stain powder in water and its penetration is increased by adding a little .880 ammonia. Water stain can be bought ready mixed in liquid form or in packets of powder. Each kind is sold in a number of shades and can be intermixed to obtain further colours.

An old-established and favourite water stain is easily made by dissolving vandyke crystals (sometimes called walnut crystals) in warm water and adding a few drops of .880 ammonia. The mixture should be strained to remove the sediment.

Bichromate of potash is another favourite water stain though in point of fact it stains by chemical reaction with the tannic acid present in the wood. It is made by shaking crystals in water until no more will dissolve—that is until the solution is saturated. This is bottled and diluted as required. Test stains are essential, for different varieties of a particular timber will react to different extents, depending upon the amount of tannic acid present in the wood. For instance, a particular solution applied to Honduras, Cuban and Spanish mahoganies will produce a much deeper red stain on the two latter woods than on the first variety. At the same time, the stain will have no effect upon deal. When using bichromate stain pay no attention to its colour (a bright orange shade). Also, work in daylight so that the produced shade can better be judged for colour. Bichromate should not be used if there are open cuts on the hands or poisoning may be set up. In other cases the mixture is quite safe.

A type of stain which is increasingly being used is aniline dye. This is obtainable in powder form in many colours and must be carefully used as some of the colours are violent in hue and may produce startling results! The powders are made for solution in water, spirits or oil and the variety required should be stated when ordering. Thus for aniline water stain, dissolve aniline water powder in warm water, add hot glue to the mixture (about a dessertspoonful to a pint of stain), and a few drops of vinegar. Mix well and strain to remove sediment. Use the stain whilst warm. Different colours of aniline stain can be blended within the same solvent class, i.e., any two water stains will blend, but a water and an oil stain will not.

Spirit Stains.

Spirit stains can only be recommended with reserve as they have a tendency to fade and require skilful handling. They do, however, have an advantage where a small surface has to be treated or where a previous finish has been cleaned off. Aniline dyes are the best type to use and aniline spirit powder will be required. This is dissolved in methylated spirits and strained through muslin. To bind the stain, add a dessertspoonful of french polish to a pint of spirit.

Oil Stains.

These are not so penetrating as water stains but have the advantage that they do not raise the grain and also that the required shade can be quickly obtained. When oil stains are used on wood which is to be wax polished, it is essential that the stain is fixed by applying two coats of french polish before waxing. The french polish is used to prevent the wax removing the stain and not to produce a shine.

Aniline oil powder is used for making oil stain and is dissolved in turpentine which should preferably be warm. Pour the turpentine into a vessel standing in hot water whilst adding the powder—never heat it over a naked flame. Strain to remove sediment and add about a dessertspoonful of gold size to each pint of stain.

Fuming.

Although fuming is classed here as a stain it is, strictly speaking, not so. It is a method of colouring wood which depends upon the chemical reaction to ammonia gas with the tannic acid present in the wood and therefore requires special appliances. The amount by which the wood is darkened and the rate at which the process works is of course dependant on the amount of tannic acid present in the wood. This again depends upon the variety of timber used; it is therefore apparent that a job made up in mixed woods will fume to different colours.

An airtight box will be required, large enough to take the whole job which should be stood inside with all the surfaces which are to be coloured, fully exposed. Also make sure that they are free from grease or glue. A saucer of ammonia of .880 strength is placed in the box—(more than one saucer may be required if the job is large)—and the door tightly closed. A dowel made of the same wood as the item being fumed is inserted through a hole bored in the side of the box. This dowel can be withdrawn from time to time and tested to see how the fuming is progressing. To do this put a spot of linseed oil on the dowel which will then darken to the tone which has so far been produced. When the required colour is obtained, remove the item from the box and rub it all over with linseed oil. This produces the final colour, after which the work is stood aside to dry.

This process is used mostly for oak which is rich in tannin. White oak turns to a grey colour in the ammonia gas and changes to rich brown when rubbed with linseed oil. Chesnut also takes on a rich colour when treated in this way whilst walnut and mahogany are less affected. The process may be hastened by coating the item with a solution of 1 oz. tannin powder dissolved in 1 quart water. Alternatively 3/4 oz. pyrogallic acid mixed in 1 quart water can be used and generally produces a more reddish tone than the former solution. By mixing the two solutions and then coating the item, intermediate shades can be produced.

If the fuming process appears to stop, it is because the ammonia gas has all been liberated, leaving plain water in the saucers. Re-start the process by substituting fresh saucers of .880 ammonia. The time occupied by the process will vary from four or five hours to a couple of days and depends on the colour required, size of box, amount of ammonia and variety of wood being treated.

APPLYING THE STAIN.

Water stains are applied with a medium-sized brush, charging it fairly full but on no account should it be dripping. Work quickly with the grain, covering just enough surface as can be conveniently treated at a time and applying the stain as evenly as possible. Wipe off with a soft rag, working along the grain. This evens the colour and takes out any accidentally made lines. Ammonia bound stains and bichromate of potash 'bite' quickly and it is very easy to leave streaks or marks caused by careless sweeps of the rag. Remember not to use bichromate if there are open cuts on the hands. When staining, leave the most important parts until last. If these are splashed with stain it is easier to clean off the marks than when the parts themselves have already been stained. Speed of working is a very important factor and on no account should the edge be allowed to dry before the next 'strip' of stain is put on.

Oil stains are applied with wadding and are simpler to handle than water stains as they do not bite so quickly. At the same time it is still, important to work quickly and evenly and not to let the edge dry. After the stain has dried it is 'washed in' by applying a coat of polish on new wadding. Do not use too much polish and work straight up and down the grain. When the filler is applied it will lighten the stain a little unless the polish coat has been put on. This may be used to advantage if the stain has been made a little too dark, for by omitting the polish, the filler can be allowed to lighten the effect.

Spirit stains dry quickly and are therefore the most difficult type to use. It is necessary to work extremely rapidly as an edge will often dry out before the next strip can be covered. This type of stain is therefore used chiefly where the surface is small and thus can be quickly covered. A cool atmosphere is an advantage as it tends to lessen the speed with which the stain dries.

STAINING CARVINGS AND END GRAIN.

In general, carvings are classed with end grain, for both easily soak up the stain and thus absorb more than their share. This produces a darker shade but can be counteracted by using a weaker stain than the body of the job. It should be applied with a brush, for if wadding is used the end grain tends to fluff the wadding and hairs, etc., become left behind and may be trapped with the filler and polish coats.

MATCHING THE STAIN.

Having stained the job, stand it in a position similar to that which it will occupy in use and examine it for evenness of tone. You will probably be surprised to find that horizontal rails appear to be lighter than vertical parts and this is due to the way in which the light falls on the grain. These light parts are now gone over once more, using a weak solution of the stain. Endeavour to match up the tone as evenly as possible for by doing so it is quite possible to miss out the colouring stage described later on. Parts which are too dark can often be lightened by rubbing over with a piece of wadding dipped in the stain solvent. Thus water is used for water stains, turpentine for oil stains, etc. Very dark patches can be treated by local brushing with a solution of oxalic acid crystals dissolved in hot water. Several applications may be needed and the solution acts as a bleacher. When the stain has been sufficiently lightened wipe over the patch with clean water, making sure that all the bleacher is removed. If any is left on it will attack the finish applied later.

FILLING THE GRAIN.

This process is not to be confused with stopping, which was used to fill holes and blemishes in the wood. Filling is used, literally, to fill the grain of the wood and was originally done by gradually working in french polish and cutting the excess off the top of the grain with glasspaper. In this way the crevices in the grain were gradually filled until a level flat surface was produced. It will at once be realised that this is a lengthy process and wastes a good deal of polish as the great majority is removed with glasspaper. Nowadays a separate filling stage is used in which various substances are worked into the grain until the surface is made level and ready for the polishing stages. Three types of filler are in general use—plaster, paste and polish-chalk. Their details are as follows:—

Plaster filler is the kind most frequently used in the cabinetmaking trade. Superfine grade plaster-of-paris will be required and for light woods is used without any tinting. Rose pink plaster-of-paris is used for filling mahogany but for medium coloured woods or where stain has been used, white plaster is toned with a little powder colour thoroughly mixed in with the dry plaster. If the wood is very dark, use a rag damped with water stain of the required shade.

Shake the plaster into a saucer and have a bowl of water or a shallow tin of stain handy. Take a piece of loosely woven canvas or hessian, damp it with water or stain and dip it into the plaster. Rub the plaster into the grain, working the canvas in small circles and using a moderate pressure. Make sure that the entire surface is covered but do not use more plaster than is really needed. Do not attempt to cover too large an area at a time. As soon as it can be seen that the plaster is setting, take a clean piece of canvas and rub firmly *across* the grain to remove the excess plaster on the surface. Do not rub with the grain or the plaster already there will be pulled out. All corners or mouldings should be cleaned out with a sharpened stick or a dry scrubbing brush.

After the whole job has been covered in this way it will appear to have a film all over it, clearly showing the path of the canvas. Make sure that the plaster is quite dry then go over the surface with a piece of cotton-wool soaked in linseed oil. If light wood and untinted plaster has been used, white mineral oil should be substituted for linseed oil. This will kill the whiteness of the plaster (unless it has already been tinted) and will leave a thin film of oil all over the job. Now rub down with glasspaper which will cause the oil to combine with the surplus plaster to form a thick paste. This in turn is wiped off with a clean rag and the job is left to dry out.

Paste fillers are generally of the proprietary type and can be had in various colours. These stain the wood and at the same time fill the grain and are applied in a similar way as plaster filler. Be sure to clean off the surface of the wood after the filler has been worked into the grain and allow at least 12 hours for the work to dry before proceeding with the next stage. If the colour of the filler is not quite right for the job it can be toned with oil stain.

The cheapness of these paste fillers makes it hardly worth while making up a filler of one's own. However, for readers who would like to do so, the following recipe will be found suitable:—

Tone some whiting with powder, colour until the desired

shade is reached. Add turpentine and mix to form a paste. To each 1 lb. of paste add a tablespoonful of gold size.

Polish chalk filler is perhaps the most simply made type and consists merely of adding about a handful of french chalk to a pint of french polish. Keep the mixture well stirred, as the chalk settles extremely quickly and apply the filler with a brush. Allow the work to dry and then ease down with No. '0' glasspaper. This filler sets hard and the glasspapering leaves a beautifully smooth surface.

FRENCH POLISHING - II

FADDING

FADDING is the first of the actual polishing stages and therefore an appropriate point at which to examine the four kinds of french polish in general use.

First, then, let us dispel one of the myths that french polish is some wonderful substance, the exact recipe of which is known only to few people and is a jealously guarded secret. It is nothing of the sort and consists merely of shellac dissolved in methylated spirit. Nothing else is added—not even a muttered incantation!

Why, then, are there different kinds of french polish? The answer is simply that they employ different kinds of shellac in order to produce different colours of polish. Here is a list of french polishes, their use and how they are made:—

White Polish is almost colourless and is used over unstained wood where a very light finish is required. It is made by dissolving 6 to 8 oz. of bleached shellac in 1 pint of methylated spirits.

Orange Polish is a pale yellow colour and is used over unstained wood or where a very light stain has been used. This is made by dissolving 6 oz. of orange shellac in 1 pint of methylated spirits.

Button Polish is a golden brown colour and is used to obtain a warm golden shade on oak or unstained walnut. It is harder than the other polishes but suffers from the disadvantage that it is inclined to be cloudy and particularly if used over dark stains, will give a muddy appearance to the work. To make this polish, dissolve 6 oz. of button shellac in 1 pint of methylated spirits.

Garnet Polish is a rich greenish-brown colour and is used over darkly stained woods. It is made by dissolving 6 oz. garnet shellac in 1 pint of methylated spirit.

When making up the polish, whatever its colour, put the shellac and spirits in a tightly corked bottle and leave it for several days until the shellac has dissolved. From time to time give the bottle a shake to assist in the dissolving process.

Any of the polishes first mentioned may be mixed together to produce intermediate shades.

You will have noticed that nothing has been said about the 'amateur' french polishes which are available. For serious work these are best avoided as they invariably contain certain gummy substances and ingredients calculated to cheapen the cost of the polish and produce a shine with the minimum of effort. For unimportant work they certainly have their uses but the finish obtained cannot be compared with that of true french polishing.

The polish is kept in a bottle and two corks will be needed. One is used in the normal way but when the polish is being used, a special cork is substituted for the normal one. This special cork has a fairly deep V-shaped groove cut in it, the object being to allow the polish to be tipped out on to the rubber as required. This will avoid tipping out too much polish at a time and either soaking the rubber or splashing the work—or both!

The next thing we shall require is some wadding for making fads and rubbers. Unbleached wadding is the kind needed, as bleached wadding or medicated cotton wool are useless. When soaked in polish these pack into a solid mass and are completely unresponsive to small changes in the pressure of the fingers which are made in the polishing operations.

The fad is merely a piece of wadding folded up into a pear shape. To make it, cut the wadding into an 8 inch square, soak it in polish and allow it to dry. This will ensure that the surface fluff and hairs are fixed to the wadding and will not pull off with use. Re-soften the fad with spirits and squeeze out the surplus. Now fold it in half and then in three, rather like the way in which a double sheet of notepaper is folded for posting. This will give the shape shown at Fig. 8*A*. Next fold down the top corners to produce *B* and then the bottom corners are folded up to make *C*. Knead the fad in the fingers to form *D*, which is the final shape.

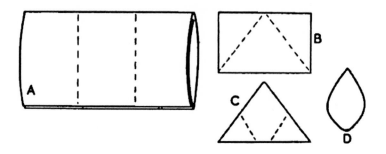

FIG. 8. FOLDING THE FAD.

Pour some polish on to the fad, making it fairly wet but on no account dripping. When squeezed lightly between the fingers the polish should exude but not run out. Tap the sole of the fad once or twice on a piece of brown paper. This flattens it and distributes the polish throughout the fad. No cover is required as the fad is used just as it is, straight on the wood. When the fad needs recharging it can either be done by pouring on more polish or by dipping the fad into some polish which has been poured into a shallow tin. This is called 'dipping-up' the fad and is only used at this stage of the work.

The purpose of fadding is to ensure that the timber is completely sealed ready for the following stages of polishing.

No oil is used on the rubber, during the first two or three coats or it may easily be trapped in the pores of the wood underneath the layer of shellac. If this happens it will subsequently migrate up through the shellac layer causing cracks and thus spoiling the finish. Work the fad backwards and forwards straight along the grain, covering the wood completely and making the coat as even as possible. Dip-up the fad as it works dry but avoid leaving streaks or ridges of wet polish behind the fad. The first coat will dry out in a few moments and the surface is then gone over with No. 0 glasspaper to remove any traces of filler which may have come up through the polish.

Repeat this process once or twice to make sure that the timber is properly sealed. The next job is to build up a groundwork of polish and to do this it will be necessary to use oil as a lubricant for the fad. Boiled linseed oil is generally used though if white polish is being applied to a light surface, white mineral oil should be substituted for linseed.

It must be emphasised that throughout the polishing operations, oil is used merely as a lubricant and in fact has afterwards to be completely removed. It follows, therefore, that no more oil should be applied than is absolutely necessary, for it only involves extra work in clearing it away.

Dip up the fad and scatter a drop or two of oil on the surface of the work. Run the fad over the wood, collecting the oil and spreading it all over the surface. It will show as a smear behind the rubber when the work is viewed by looking across the surface against the light. A little more oil can be added if required to make sure that the whole surface is covered. During this process the fad is moved up and down the grain but when the surface is entirely covered with the oil smear, change the movement to the fairly large circles shown at Fig. 9 *A*. Notice that the main part of the work is treated in circles whilst the edges are covered by working figures-of-eight. Work over the surface in this way, dipping up the fad as required. A little more pressure can now be used on the fad, for the oil acts as a lubricant. If bright streaks show when a newly dipped-up fad is used, apply a spot of oil to the face and continue working. As soon as it can be seen that the polish is being built up on the surface of the wood, change the movement of the fad to large figures-of-eight as shown in sketch *B*. The object is to spread the polish evenly over the entire surface and the way in which this is being done will be shown by the oil smear. At this stage the surface should be dulled, rather like glass which has been breathed on, and the path of the rubber should be clearly seen. Watch for any pimples which may have formed on the surface. These are caused by particles of dust or fluff settling on the surface and being covered with polish, which builds up into the pimple. They should be eased down with a piece of worn No. 0 glasspaper which has been lightly smeared with oil.

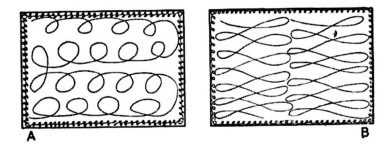

FIG. 9. MOVEMENT OF THE FAD.

We have now finished with the fad and will be using a rubber for the succeeding stages of the work. The only difference between a rubber and a fad is that the former is covered with material. To make the rubber, cut an 8 inch square of wadding and fold it exactly as though making a fad. Charge it with polish, pouring this on to the back of the wadding and then cover with cloth. The best type of cloth to use is an old washed-out linen handkerchief or some similar material which is completely free of fluff. Coloured rags, silks, etc., should not be used.

There are right and wrong ways of covering the rubber and the best method is shown in Fig. 10. The object is to produce a perfectly smooth covering at the undersurface which is quite free from wrinkles and at the same time to preserve the pointed shape. Just screwing up the wadding in the cloth is no help at all. It only has the effect of making the contact surface into a disc which, being smaller than the rubber, decreases its effective size. More important, though, is the fact that the polish gets squeezed out to the edges of the disc and is very easily left as liquid streaks on the work.

Cut a piece of material about 8 inches square and place the wadding as shown in Fig. 10*A*. Next hold with the left hand as in sketch *B* whilst the fingers of the right hand press the point of the wadding up to the cloth and at the same time draw it close over the face. Nip the point of the rubber lightly between the fingers of the left hand as at *C*, folding the material back from the point as shown. Next fold again so that the edge lies along the left hand side of the rubber as shown at *D*. Next hold the rubber as shown at *E* with the forefinger holding the front part of the cloth over the pad and the rest of the material lightly nipped under the thumb. Take the rubber in the left hand and 'screw' it round in an anticlockwise direction. This wraps the rest of the material round and forms the final shape as shown at *F*. All this sounds a little involved but is perfectly easy to do and produces a neatly made rubber, which is essential if good work is to be done with it.

Referring back to Fig. 9, we have to continue with the movements shown in *B*, using a little oil as required, then change to that shown at 11*A*. The oil now has to be renewed in order that the shellac may dry out evenly. Re-charge the rubber and use a fresh cover but do not apply any oil. Work again as at *A*, using a light touch and keeping the rubber on the work. Bright streaks will appear, which indicate that the oil is being taken off. It may be necessary to re-charge the rubber but do not do so until it is nearly dry. The final strokes are made as shown at *B*, where the rubber is taken straight up and down the grain and completely leaves the wood at each end. It is most important that when starting the rubber on the wood at each stroke, it is not deliberately put down on the edge, or the polish will lump up and may even drip over the corner. It should be glided on to the work so that excess polish is not scraped off the rubber by the square edge of the wood.

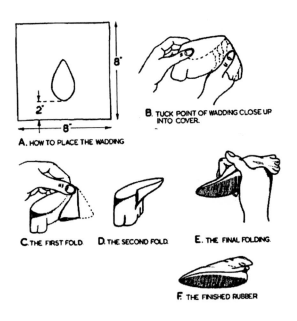

A. HOW TO PLACE THE WADDING

B. TUCK POINT OF WADDING CLOSE UP INTO COVER.

C. THE FIRST FOLD

D. THE SECOND FOLD

E. THE FINAL FOLDING.

F. THE FINISHED RUBBER

FIG. 10. HOW TO MAKE THE POLISHING RUBBER.

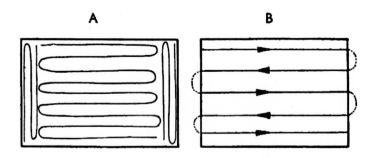

FIG. 11. MOVEMENTS OF THE BODYING RUBBER.

The surface should now have a fair polish and this is left to thoroughly harden before the next stage is commenced.

FRENCH POLISHING - III

COLOURING

THE object of this process is to even the colour of the parts and, if necessary, to tone the whole job to the exact shade which is required. Some readers may at once say that surely this was the object of staining the work. Agreed, in the staining process every precaution is taken to obtain evenness of colour but all the same there is nearly always an odd patch here and there which requires further treatment. At the same time stain looks different under a coat of polish and now that the oil has been taken off the fadding coat, the colour may not be quite right.

The materials required for colouring are as follows:—

1. Colour brush.

2. Pencil brush.

3. Powder colours (various).

4. Spirit dyes (various).

For the colour brush, a No. 6 quill bound camel hair mop will be needed, and it is best to avoid cheap ones—they have a distressing habit of shedding hairs even though they have been 'fixed' as described later. The pencil brush should also be of good quality, the cheaper kind will not form to the delicate point which will be required.

Before the brushes are used, suspend them in polish for a day or so to set the hairs. Then take them out, squeeze out the excess polish and let them dry. For the first few occasions they are used, soften them in polish—later on spirits can be used for softening as by this time the polish in the roots of the hair will have set quite hard.

Place the work in a similar position to that which it will normally occupy, i.e., either horizontally or vertically. As explained before, in the staining process, it is necessary to do this as the angle at which the light falls on the grain has a marked influence on its apparent colour.

For purposes of description we will assume that our practice piece of wood has certain irregularities of colour. A long streak of lighter tone, several patches about the size of a half-crown and a few tiny spots all need touching up.

First make up a half strength polish, that is, half polish and half spirits. To this add a pinch of powder colour, stirring well and making the polish up to the same general *colour* although a lighter *shade* than that of the wood. Cut off a piece of an old fad—quite a small piece will do—say about the size of half-a-crown. Flatten it out and charge it by dipping the colour brush in the polish and applying it to the fad. Also put just the lightest touch of oil on the surface of the fad. Now, starting with the light streak, glide on the fad and work it lightly up and down, following the streak and taking care not to go over the darker places. Touch up the larger patches in the same way. The small spots are treated with the pencil brush and this is dipped into the polish, half squeezed out and brought to a point in the fingers. Just touch the brush over the spots and apply the thinnest coat possible or it will show through the subsequent layers of polish as a raised patch.

Patches which are too small to be comfortably dealt with by the colour fad, yet too large to tackle with the pencil brush are treated with the colour brush. This is also used for mouldings and where, say, the rail of a carcase has to be coloured. Here the main part of the rail is worked over with the fad whilst the brush can be taken right into the corner angle.

It is unlikely that the patches will be completely coloured in a single application, but the polish must be allowed to thoroughly dry before another treatment is given. If this is not done, the second lot of polish will merely soften and amalgamate with the first and when you have 'finished' this second application you will, in reality, only have put on one coat!

Having treated the patches, streaks and spots and evened up the colouring, you must now decide whether the overall tone of the job is just what is required. Remember that the coats of polish applied in the next stage (that of bodying-up) will slightly darken the finish, but only to a limited extent. Assuming, however, that the overall tone needs to be darkened, this is done with the colour fad. Charge a piece of old fad with the colour polish, apply a spot of oil to it and work lightly over the surface. Follow the grain as closely as possible as the colour fad leaves fairly easily defined lines in its wake. On variegated grain and if the fad were taken straight up and down the wood, these streaks of colour would show up quite plainly and spoil the look of the job. The most important things, therefore, are to use a weak colour and to follow the grain so far as can be done.

It sometimes happens that the colour is dark enough in tone but the actual shade is not quite right. For instance, a piece of mahogany may have been stained too red and needs to be made a less fiery colour. This can be done by going over the work with a fad charged with polish which has been tinted with spirit yellow or green. Spirit soluble dyes are used and should be made very weak—say about a pinch of colour to a pint of polish. Be sure not to make the colour too strong,—it is much better to apply two or even three 'pale' coats in order to reach the correct shade than to spoil the whole job with one heavily over-coloured coat.

So far we have tackled all the pale patches but have not

considered what must be done when colouring over hard stopping such as beaumontage. This, of course, was originally made up as nearly as possible to the finished colour of the job but quite possibly needs more toning. The colours used so far have been transparent but for this job we shall need a more opaque type.

For these, solid colours are used such as raw, burnt and brown umber, red lead, yellow ochre, orange chrome, etc. These can all be obtained in small quantities from the oil and colour stores. To make up the colours, put a couple of brush-fulls of polish on to a piece of brown paper and with the brush damp but not wet, pick up a little of the solid colour and work it into the polish in the manner of mixing colour on a palette. Do not make the colour too thick but get it to the right shade, then touch out the patches with the pencil brush. Allow the colour to dry, then mix a little darker colour and with an almost dry brush, stroke in 'grain' marks over the previous colouring so as to merge the patch into the surrounding wood.

This treatment can also successfully be used on plywood edgings. The edge is first smoothed and is then well rubbed over with beeswax. This is papered down and the background colour laid on and allowed to dry. The graining is then done with the pencil brush and allowed to dry.

In all cases, the colouring should be fixed by giving the

work a coat of polish, using a new clean rubber. It must be applied lightly or the colouring may be lifted off. For the same reason the job should be done quickly and not gone over more than once.

When finished with the brushes, they should always be washed out. If polish colour has been used, wash out the brushes in polish, point the hairs in the fingers and allow to dry. This keeps the brush in shape and when next it is required it can be softened in spirits. If solid colour has been used, the brush must be washed out in spirits for if it is left to harden with the solid colour still in the hairs, the brush will be ruined.

FRENCH POLISHING - IV

BODYING

THIS stage of the work consists of building up a clear and even film of shellac to an appreciable thickness and a good finish cannot be obtained unless this is properly done.

At this stage the 'pull' of the rubber becomes an important factor and the way in which the polish is being put on is determined by the amount of pull which exists between the rubber and the surface.

To understand this properly, let us consider for a moment what is happening. The polish consists of two ingredients, shellac and spirits. To this we are adding a third—namely oil. In its final state, french polish is merely a thin film of shellac spread evenly all over the surface. The spirits have evaporated and the oil has been removed.

We could of course dispense entirely with the oil and merely brush on the shellac and spirit mixture but in doing so we could not obtain the even, thin film of shellac which is so desirable. This is the reason why brush polishes cannot approach the finish of a properly french polished surface.

Here the shellac-spirit mixture is applied to the surface and, literally, spread evenly all over it with the rubber.

To get a clearer picture of what is involved, imagine the shellac, greatly magnified, looking like glue pearls which have been soaked in water preparatory to the boiling stage. The pearls are jellified though each is still a separate 'blob' surrounded by a gummy solution. Each 'blob' has to be spread out flat on the surface of the wood and merged with the 'blobs' which surround it so as to produce a homogeneous layer of glue.

The shellac is in a similar state, it is sticky and soft and we are proposing to spread it all over the wood with a piece of cloth wrapped around a soft pad. So long as there is a fair amount of spirit left in the polish, the cloth can slide over the shellac without much difficulty, but as soon as the spirit evaporates we are down on to the sticky shellac and, of course, there is considerable friction between this and the rubber-face.

There must, of course, be a certain amount of friction present, otherwise we cannot spread the shellac evenly, so it is obvious that the amount necessary is an important factor. The shellac particles are too small to be seen by the naked eye and we can only judge what is happening by the amount of friction or 'pull' of the rubber. When this becomes too great, due to further evaporation of the spirit, we may easily pull the shellac into humps and thus completely ruin the effect for which we are aiming. To avoid doing this we apply oil to the rubber. This will not mix with the spirits or the shellac but acts as a lubricant and by easing the passage of the rubber, prevents it pulling the shellac up into humps.

The experienced worker is familiar with the amount of pull which is required but a good way of judging this is to clean and dry a mirror, then rub the ball of the hand (which should also be dry) over the surface. A definite resistance will be felt and this is about the same as the pull on the polish rubber when the amount of oil being used is correct. More oil will lessen the pull but in any event has to be completely removed later on.

Charge the rubber so that it exudes polish when the sole is pressed but do not fill it so much that it drips. When in use the path of polish which it leaves should not have clearly defined edges or the polish may be built up into ridges. This is an infallible sign that the rubber is too full of polish.

The first movements of the bodying rubber are shown at Fig. 12.*A*, where large circles are worked over the surface and the extreme edges are 'reinforced' with lines of small circles as shown. Cover the entire surface and give special attention to the edges and corners. Increase the pressure on the rubber as the polish becomes used up and work until it is nearly dry before re-charging. When a fair thickness of polish has been built up change the movement to the large figures-of-eight shown at *B*. This is done to still further spread the polish evenly over the work. Do not neglect the edges or corners. This movement is next changed to the large ovals shown at Fig. 13*A*, which are gradually converted into the back and forth sweeps of *B*.

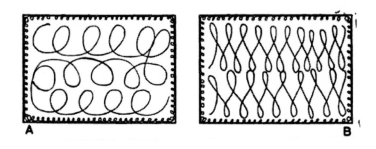

FIG. 12. MOVEMENT OF THE BODYING RUBBER.

The purpose behind the circular movements is to 'pull over' the polish, which, when laid on by the movements with the grain, tends to form into ridges. The transverse movements of the rubber thus take polish off the tops of these ridges and spread it into the hollows. Sometimes, particularly if the polish has been too liberally applied, these ridges become quite well defined and are known as 'whips'. Difficulty is often experienced in pulling over the polish and thus smoothing them down. Matters can be helped by using what is known as a 'grinder'. This is simply a polish rubber which has had a pinch of the finest pumice powder spread over the sole, *underneath* the covering linen. The grinder must, of course, not be used for any other purpose.

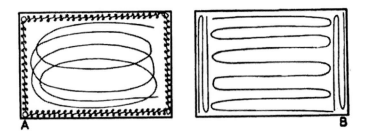

FIG. 13. BODYING RUBBER MOVEMENTS.

The final stage of the bodying coat is to go over the surface with a new rubber and without using any oil. The rubber is taken straight up and down and should be only lightly charged. The object is to remove the oil from the surface and this will be apparent by bright streaks being left behind the rubber. Keep the head low and look across the work at an angle towards the light. If the rubber shows traces of leaving an oil smear, move the cloth round so that the wadding is covered with a fresh surface. When quite clear of oil, leave the surface for at least 24 hours to harden. In this stage it should have an appreciable shine and be quite free from smears.

Two or even three more bodying coats will probably be required to build up a good depth of polish. Commence each one by going over the surface with a piece of old No. 0 grade glasspaper which has been lightly smeared with oil. Wipe off well with clean rag and then put on the body coat. At the last application, leave on the oil, for we shall then be ready for the finishing stage.

FRENCH POLISHING - V

STIFFING AND SPIRITING OFF

TWO methods of finishing the work will be described, namely stiffing and spiriting-off. There is a third method in which acid is used to clear the surface but so far as the amateur is concerned this is perhaps best left alone.

In both stiffing and spiriting off, the object is to clear the remainder of the oil smear left after the final bodying coat and therefore follows immediately upon the process, without waiting for the polish to harden.

STIFFING.

The rubber used for this process should preferably be one which was newly made up for the final bodying coat. On no account should a grinder be used and if a bodying rubber is not available, make up a new one, apply one bodying coat and go straight on to the stiffing.

Charge the rubber to about half the content used for bodying—(known as a half-strength rubber)—but do not apply any oil. Starting from the far edge of the work glide the rubber on and work straight along the surface and off the end. Now return, making the stroke overlap the first one and continue in this way. The oil smear will be gradually reduced and as it does, the pull of the rubber will increase. Be careful to work straight up and down the surface, for if the rubber is allowed to travel in an arc, the marks will show in the finished job.

The rubber must be lightly used and the more delicate the touch, the better will be the results. Do not charge the rubber too much or ridges of polish may be left which will ruin the finish. When the surface is quite clear, stand the work aside for two or three days to set quite hard before it is used.

SPIRITING OFF.

This follows immediately upon the bodying stage and the rubber is charged half with spirits and half with polish and is thus referred to as a half-and-half rubber. There will probably be sufficient oil on the surface to lubricate the rubber and none should be added unless really necessary. Work in large circles, changing to ovals and then long straight turns until the rubber is quite dry. At this stage the oil smear should be very faint and only apparent when the surface is viewed at an angle towards the light.

To remove the last of the smear and to burnish the surface

of the polish, the work is gone over with a spirit rubber. This consists of an old rubber washed out in spirits until quite free of polish, remade and covered with fine-textured linen. To charge the rubber, dip it into a few drops of spirit which have been sprinkled in the palm of the hand. Test by holding it against the lips, when it should just feel cold, indicating that spirit is present but not in sufficient quantity to feel wet. Too much spirit will soften the polish and may even cause it to be pulled up by the rubber. It is best to err on the dry side for if so the oil smear will not be taken right off but will look as though dry cloth is being rubbed over it.

Take the spirit rubber straight up and down the work making sure that the entire surface is treated evenly. Bright streaks will appear in the wake of the rubber, indicating that the oil is being taken off. Continue until the rubber is quite dry, when the surface should have a really good gloss. For a final burnish dip the rubber into some Vienna chalk and work up and down the surface as before, then stand the work aside for a few days to thoroughly harden off.

———————

That is all there is to french polishing and provided the stages have been methodically worked, the practice pieces should each have a good surface, able to stand comparison with any well-finished, professionally made furniture. If this is not so, go back over the processes in your mind, criticising honestly and fairly to decide just where the errors crept in.

You may be quite sure that an unsatisfactory finish is the result of one or more of the processes not being properly carried out, for as stated earlier, all the necessary information has been given and no tricks or processes, which are vital to the job, have been withheld. Maybe you are fairly satisfied with the results obtained but these still fall short of a really first class finish. In this case the remedy is to practice further and thus obtain the proficiency required before tackling furniture jobs.

FRENCH POLISHING - IV

EBONISED AND IVORY FINISH EBONISING.

EBONISING, when properly done, produces a rich deep black surface full of lustre and of dignified appearance. Although it is hardly suited to modern colour schemes, the present day trend of unbroken flat surfaces provides ideal opportunities to use this type of finish for small items. Thus a perfectly plain item such as a cigarette box can be given the appearance almost of opulence by this finish. One important point must be made before proceeding further and that is the problem of corners. For work which is to be ebonised, all corners should be given a slight radius, but sufficient to take off the dead squareness. The reason is that corners come in for a good deal of wear during dusting operations and if they are dead square, the ebony finish is soon removed. First they become a browny tone, soon followed by a light streak where the polish has completely worn through. By taking off the absolute squareness, wear is reduced and the problem largely overcome.

Almost any close grained wood can successfully be

ebonised—cherry, pear, birch, beech and black walnut are very suitable whilst American whitewood has a suitable surface but being rather soft is liable to become bruised. Avoid using oak, ash and teak. The first two are naturally open grained woods and need a lot of filling which is susceptible to sinking. Teak has a natural greasiness which prevents the stain going on evenly. Mahogany is often used but take care to choose a variety with a fine close grain.

Prepare the surface in the normal way but be careful to scrape off all tears and give the work a thorough rub down with grade 'o' or even finer glasspaper. Next swab the whole surface with water containing a teaspoonful of common soda to each pint of water. This removes any trace of grease and at the same time raises the grain. Rub down once more and dust off the surface.

The next job is to stain the surface and for this one of the proprietary makes of ebony or black water stains can be used. An alternative method is to make up a stain with water soluble aniline black powder dye. Mix with warm water and add a little scotch glue to act as a binder and a few drops of ammonia to help drive the stain into the grain. Another good stain consists of drop-black—(bought in the form of a thick paste)—thinned with turpentine and having 1/2 oz. gold size added to each pint of the mixture to act as a binder.

Apply a coat of stain and allow the work to dry out. Next

paper down any roughness, using fine grade paper, preferably worn, and being careful not to go right through the stain at the corners. Apply a second coat of stain and again allow to dry.

Filling the grain is the next operation and if an oil stain has been used a proprietary brand of black paste filler should be employed. Where the aniline or other water stain, has been used, the grain is filled with plaster. To make the filler, mix a little plaster with lamp black. The latter is bought as a powder from the colourman. Instead of using water, the plaster is applied on a rag dipped in the aniline stain, which should be re-warmed for the purpose. Rub the filler well into the grain, wipe off all surplus and stand the work aside to dry. Then go over the job with a rag moistened with linseed oil. This will pick up any loose filler on the surface and turn it into mud which is easily wiped away with a clean rag. After this process the work is again allowed to dry thoroughly before commencing to polish.

The polishing operations are exactly the same as for ordinary french polishing. Fadding, bodying and spiriting out are tackled in the normal way but of course the colouring stage will not be required. You will need a supply of black polish and this can either be bought ready mixed or can be made up at home. To do so, dissolve 1/2 oz. spirit soluble black aniline dye in I pint white french polish, mixing well together.

Now take a piece of washing blue—(the familiar housewives' blue-bag)—wrap it in a scrap of muslin and dip it into about a teaspoonful of methylated spirits which have been poured into an egg-cup. Squeeze out the bag once or twice so that a little of the blue is dissolved and stir this well into the polish. This helps to give the black polish a more intense shade. Before use, the polish should be strained through fine muslin to remove any sediment or undissolved powder.

Using the black polish is a mucky job at the best of times and it is unavoidable that the fingers get badly stained. Matters can be helped by having a jar containing methylated spirits and an old tooth-brush handy. From time to time as the work proceeds, scrub the fingers with the tooth-brush and spirits—this will help to get rid of the stain. Various barrier creams are made for use before doing dirty jobs but these should not be employed when french polishing. They all contain grease and are only efficient providing the fingers and hands are well covered with cream. This of course means that if the work is touched with the finger, grease will be deposited and will ruin the finish.

Having polished the surface, the result will be a brilliant gloss and whilst this is admittedly attractive, it is not a characteristic ebony finish, which is a fine eggshell texture. To produce such a surface, the gloss is scratched! This is done with superfine grade pumice powder applied with a brush.

A wide fairly soft brush is required and is dipped into the powder and drawn in straight lines along the surface of the wood. This produces very fine scratches and converts the high gloss to an attractive sheen.

It is of course most important that the brush strokes are perfectly straight and they must not be gone over a second time. A little practice before actually doing the work is advisable in order to obtain the required control over the brush. A good plan to ensure straight brushwork is to use a batten as shown in Fig. 14, for a guide strip. This batten has a strip of felt or soft rag pinned to it so that the glossy surface will not be spoilt. It is most important that the batten is never placed over any part of the surface which has been dulled, or particles of pumice will be embedded in the covering and thus produce unwanted scratches.

FIG. 14. DULLING THE EBONISED SURFACE.

IVORY FINISH.

An attractive treatment for very light woods which is becoming increasingly popular at the present time is the ivory white finish. It is often seen on white birch, sycamore, etc. Where the wood is sufficiently light it is treated by french polishing with white or transparent white polish. The polish itself is used as a filler and will therefore need more fadding coats than usual. White mineral oil should be used as a lubricant in place of linseed. The eggshell gloss finish looks well for such a scheme and can be produced by the brush and pumice method as described for ebonising.

In some cases the wood is not sufficiently white in its original state and therefore needs to be lightened. This is done at the fadding stage by adding powdered chinese white to the white polish. Only just sufficient powder should be added so that when the polish is put on, the solid colour just shows. It must on no account be overdone or the white in the polish will cloud over the grain and produce a 'painted' effect. At the same time the effect of the polish cannot be properly judged until it has dried and for this reason it will be necessary to try it out on a specimen piece of the wood in order to get the right mix. The stages of the work are just the same as for normal french polishing.

FRENCH POLISHING - VII

FAULTS AND HOW TO AVOID THEM

'Chinese Writing.'

THIS fault appears to be similar to sweating, except that the cracks are usually very fine and run in all directions. Frequently a considerable area of the surface is covered in these cracks to produce an irregular mosaic effect. Once this fault has appeared there is no cure and the only thing to do is to strip right down to the wood and repolish entirely. 'Chinese writing' is caused by one or more coats of polish drying unevenly. The contraction of the polish film being uneven causes the layer to split up into separate particles grouped around the areas of greatest shrinking. To avoid this fault use good quality polish and—what is more important—use the same polish throughout the work. This is because two dissimilar brands of polish, though each of good quality, may have different drying contraction factors. As the rate at which french polish dries is comparatively slow it is not practical to wait until a particular coat is dead hard right through, before applying the next. Thus if a first body coat is applied using polish having a high contraction factor and a second body coat of a 'lower contraction' polish, the underneath coat when finally hardened will have split the upper coat into 'Chinese writing.'

Clouded Surface.

A fault sometimes called 'bloom' though the latter term is more applicable to varnished work affected in this way. White streaks may also be present which are due to the same cause, namely moisture becoming trapped in the polish. To avoid this trouble work in a dry, warm atmosphere. It is also an advantage to allow the work to stand for some time in the room before commencing to polish. Any surface humidity thus has a chance to evaporate before becoming trapped. It is also important to avoid working in a draught for a current of cold air striking the surface during polishing operations will cause moisture to be deposited which is immediately trapped under the surface.

Dull Surface.

More often than not this is a beginner's chief fault and is almost always due to using too much oil or not completing the spiriting out stage. Admittedly, spiriting out is a somewhat tricky process and one in which the finish can easily be ruined. It is again emphasised that the beginner cannot do better than to work on a practice piece, treating it with as much care as though it is a regular furniture item. The experience thus gained in the spiriting-out process will be invaluable.

Pimply Surface.

Here the surface is marred by 'pimples' in the shellac which may be scattered haphazardly over the job. These are caused by particles of dust settling on the 'wet' surface during polishing and becoming covered in shellac. The best way to avoid this is to work in a dust free room. The floor can be *slightly* damped down but at all costs avoid causing a humid atmosphere which may set up clouding in the polish.

Ropey Surface.

An effect produced by a series of ridges running with the grain. Caused by moving the rubber up and down the grain and neglecting the pulling over movements. Avoid the fault by proper attention to the rubber movements.

Streaky or Rough Surface.

Most usually caused by faulty surface preparations and often by omitting to raise the grain of the wood before staining. In Chapter I we dealt with the operation of raising and then cutting down the grain—if this is omitted the subsequent staining operation (particularly if water stain is used) will raise the grain and result in uneven staining.

Another cause of streaky surface is the use of varnish stains under french polish. These should never be used in such circumstances apart from their being difficult to apply in an even coat.

Streakiness may also be caused by faulty application of the polish, particularly if the various rubber movements which have been advocated are not followed. These movements are not selected haphazardly but are those which have for years been proved to obtain an even distribution of polish throughout the work. The remarks in Chapter V about spreading the polish over the work and the allusion to spreading glue, should be studied, for it is only by thoroughly understanding the reasons for the rubber movements that an even coat of polish can be obtained.

A further cause of streaky results lies in uneven filling or in failing to seal the grain before filling. If the grain has been sealed (as it always should be)—but the filler is unevenly applied it is obvious that those parts of the surface where the filler is sparse or non-existent will absorb more polish than others. Whilst covered, the true surface of the polish will exhibit slight hollows which are merely accentuated as a higher gloss is built up.

If the grain has not been sealed, the worker is heading for trouble right from the outset. The reason is because wood does not absorb polish at an even rate all over the surface, thus in some parts the polish will soak into the grain whilst in others it will lie on the top surface and a streaky or patchy result is inevitable.

Sweating.

This fault usually develops some little time after the item has been polished and appears in the form of a number of cracks which develop in the polish film as distinct from the wood. The cause is due to oil which has been imprisoned under one or more layers of shellac and subsequently migrated to the surface. The only true remedy is an Irish one—and that is not to cause the fault to develop! Sweating is caused, in the great majority of cases, by failure to remove the oil smear between the polishing stages. Unless this is properly done, the fresh coat of shellac imprisons the oil and the foundation is laid for subsequent sweating.

Whips.

Curved ridges of polish caused by using the rubber too wet and failing to flatten out by proper rubber movements.

Lightning Source UK Ltd.
Milton Keynes UK
UKOW03f1102040417
298306UK00001B/69/P

9 781447 444423